5 √

1/95

J Mankiller
13.28
12/94

To the Reader…

Our purpose in creating this series is to provide young readers with accurate accounts of the lives of Native American men and women important in the history of their tribes. The stories are written by scholars, including American Indians.

Native Americans are as much a part of North American life today as they were one hundred years ago. Even in times past, Indians were not all the same. Not all of them lived in teepees or wore feather warbonnets. They were not all warriors. Some did fight against the white man, but many befriended him.

Whether patriot or politician, athlete or artist, Arapaho or Zuni, the story of each person in this series deserves to be told. Whether the individuals gained distinction on the battlefield or the playing field, in the courtroom or the classroom, they have enriched the heritage and history of all Americans. It is hoped that those who read their stories will realize that many different peoples, regardless of culture or color, have played a part in shaping the United States and Canada, in making both countries what they are today.

Herman J. Viola
General Editor
Author of *Exploring the West*
and other volumes on the West
and Native Americans

GENERAL EDITOR

Herman J. Viola

Author of *Exploring the West* and other volumes on the West
and Native Americans

MANAGING EDITOR

Robert M. Kvasnicka

Coeditor of *The Commissioners of Indian Affairs, 1824-1977*
Coeditor of *Indian-White Relations: A Persistent Paradox*

MANUSCRIPT EDITOR

Eric Newman

PROJECT MANAGER

Joyce Spicer

PRODUCTION

Jack Reichard
Scott Melcer

Published by Steck-Vaughn 1993

Copyright © 1993 Pinnacle Press, Inc., doing business as Rivilo Books

Library of Congress Cataloging-in-Publication Data

Rand, Jacki Thompson.
    Wilma Mankiller / text by Jacki Thompson Rand; illustrations by
Wayne Anthony Still.
       p.   cm. — (American Indian stories)
    "A Rivilo book."
    Summary: Describes the life of the first woman to be elected
Principal Chief of the Oklahoma Cherokees.
    ISBN 0-8114-6576-4   —   ISBN 0-8114-4097-4 (soft cover)
    1. Mankiller, Wilma Pearl, 1945 — Juvenile literature.
2. Cherokee Indians — Biography — Juvenile literature.
3. Cherokee Indians — Juvenile literature.   [1. Mankiller,
Wilma Pearl, 1945-. 2. Cherokee Indians — Biography.
3. Indians of North America — Oklahoma — Biography.]
I. Still, Wayne Anthony, ill. II. Title. III. Series.
E99.C5M336 1993
976.6'00497502 — dc20
  [B]   92-12813
                                              CIP AC

WILMA
MANKILLER

Text by Jacki Thompson Rand
Illustrations by Wayne Anthony Still

A RIVILO BOOK

**RAINTREE
STECK-VAUGHN**
P U B L I S H E R S
The Steck-Vaughn Company

In 1985 Wilma P. Mankiller made history when she became the Principal Chief of the Oklahoma Cherokees. Long ago, when all of the Cherokee people lived in the southeastern region of the United States, Cherokee women played an important role in directing the tribe's future. It was the job of the clan mothers, as they were called, to choose the leaders of the Cherokee people. Some female leaders were given the title "Beloved Woman." Until Wilma's selection, however, no woman had ever served as Principal Chief, the leader of the tribe. As in earlier times, being elected Chief of the tribe is a great honor and carries much responsibility. To today's Cherokees, the Principal Chief is their community's equivalent of the United States' president.

6

The Cherokee tribe is today one of the largest Indian tribes in the United States. Before the whites arrived, the Cherokees lived in the southern Appalachian Mountains and nearby lands in what is now Tennessee, North Carolina, Alabama, and Georgia. There they hunted and fished and raised crops for food.

In time, European colonists settled in the land of the Cherokees. They brought with them African slaves from across the Atlantic. The Cherokee society was changed forever as a result of contact with these foreigners. By the early 1800s so many whites wanted Cherokee land that the United States government forced the Indians to move. Between 1835 and 1840, the government relocated most of the Cherokees to an area called Indian Territory, now the state of Oklahoma. Today, some Cherokees live in the mountains of North Carolina, but most of the tribe lives in northeastern Oklahoma.

Wilma Mankiller was born on November 18, 1945, in Tahlequah, Oklahoma. Her father was a full-blooded Cherokee; her mother is Dutch and Irish. Mixed marriages between Indians and whites are common among the Cherokees. The Mankiller name comes from a military title used long ago and adopted by one of Wilma's ancestors. Wilma, a quiet spoken person, is very proud of her family name because it gives the impression of strength and courage.

When Wilma was a little girl she lived with her family on a 160-acre farm called Mankiller Flats located in Adair County. The farm was originally allotted to Wilma's grandfather and was later passed down to her father. The Mankiller family grew strawberries, green beans, peanuts, and other crops. They were poor farmers, but everyone helped to make the farm successful. Wilma and her sister rode horses to the freshwater spring to get water for the family. They lived simply: their home had no electricity, no indoor plumbing, no telephone, and no luxuries like television.

The Mankillers did own a battery-operated radio, and at night the family gathered around it and listened to popular programs such as comedies, dramas, and soap operas. Also, Wilma's father invented games for the children to play, and there were always lots of books to read at the Mankiller house. From spring through the fall, the family would go to Cherokee stomp dances, which are community get-togethers that last for many days and nights. Wilma's family was poor, but their life together was full of sharing in work, play, and Cherokee social activities.

One year there was very little rain. The drought brought even poorer times to the Mankiller family, which by this time included nine children. Wilma's father and her oldest brother tried to get help from the local office of the United States government's Bureau of Indian Affairs, but there were no programs to help farmers at that time. Finally, the family made the only choice that could save them from their desperate situation. They allowed the government to move them to California, where Wilma's father and brother could get jobs.

Wilma was about twelve years old then. Neither she nor her siblings wanted to leave Oklahoma. How could they move so far from home? How could they leave their friends? They wanted to run away so that they could avoid moving to the strange place called California. What, they wondered, would California be like? They were certain it would be a frightening place.

WELCOME TO CALIFORNIA

Indeed, California was very frightening for the Mankiller children. They moved to an apartment in San Francisco, where, among other strange things, they saw elevators for the first time. Wilma and the other children were terrified of this "box" that took people away and brought new ones in their place! The Mankiller children used the stairs rather than risk going into the box that took people away.

The Mankiller children were strangers in this new place. For the first time in their lives, they were different from everyone else. When they spoke, their twangy Oklahoma accents let all the other schoolchildren know that they did not come from California. Wilma and her brothers and sisters, anxious to gain acceptance by the other children, struggled unsuccessfully to lose their accents.

Life in California could be wonderful, too. For the first time, the Mankiller children rode bicycles and talked on the telephone.

Despite the wondrous new experiences, Wilma still missed her relatives and friends back in Oklahoma. When she found herself getting homesick, she would recall stories her great-aunt, Maggie Mankiller Gourd, had told her. One story explained why the front door to her great-aunt's house was scarred. Aunt Maggie had gone to bed and dreamed that wild bison roamed near her house. For some unknown reason the bison were angry with her, and during the night they charged at her front door. When Aunt Maggie awoke in the morning, she found the marks and gashes in the front door of her house. For Wilma and her brothers and sisters, it was a wonderfully frightening story that had brought excitement to their lives in Adair County. Later, in San Francisco, the story brought comfort to a young girl far from home.

Wilma grew up in California. Then, like many other young women who did not go to college right after high school, Wilma married at an early age. Her husband was a young man from the country of Ecuador, in South America. They had two daughters, Gina and Felicia.

In 1969 something happened that changed the course of Wilma's life. During the 1960s many young people all over the United States began to voice their concerns about many social problems. Young Native American people also began to express their anger over the treatment, past and present, of American Indians and to demand improvements in their communities. They formed the American Indian Rights movement. In November 1969 young Indians from many tribes, including the Cherokees, occupied the empty prison buildings on Alcatraz Island in San Francisco Bay. The prison had been closed in 1963. The Indians hoped that taking the prison would give them the chance to make the public aware of how bad conditions were for their people.

Wilma shared the feelings of the young Native American demonstrators. Because she had to care for her daughters, she could not join the Indians in their vigil on the island, but she wanted to help them however she could. So she helped raise money to support them. The Indians held the prison for nineteen months, until June 1971, when law-enforcement officers removed them from the island.

In 1970 another event that would have an important effect on Wilma's future took place in Washington, D.C. That year, the United States Congress passed a law allowing the Cherokee tribe in Oklahoma to establish an elected tribal government. The Cherokees could elect a Principal Chief, a Deputy Principal Chief, and a fifteen-member tribal council to pass tribal laws. Elections were to be held every four years.

Wilma spent much of her time thinking about her people and ways in which she might help them. She began taking classes at San Francisco State University. She also got a job with the Oakland, California, public school system, working on Native American programs.

Wilma had two goals. She wanted to continue her college education, and she wanted to return to Oklahoma, where she could work to make conditions better for her tribe. Because Wilma's life was changing so rapidly, she could no longer maintain the traditional marriage that her husband desired. Wilma and her husband divorced. In 1976 she and her daughters moved back to Mankiller Flats, the family farm in Oklahoma. There she built a new house.

Wilma moved quickly to accomplish her other goals. She got an administrative job with the tribal government of the Cherokee Nation, and she graduated in 1978 from Flaming Rainbow University with a degree in social science. Still wanting more education, Wilma decided to work toward a degree in community planning. She began attending graduate school at the University of Arkansas.

She was driving to school one day when she was involved in a very serious car accident. Her car was so badly wrecked that people were amazed she survived the crash. The driver of the other car was killed, and Wilma was severely injured. Her left leg and some of her ribs were broken, and her right leg and bones in her face were crushed. Seventeen operations were required to repair her injuries. Wilma had to work very hard to recover.

While she was still recovering from the car accident, Wilma learned that she had a serious disease called myasthenia gravis, a form of muscular dystrophy. Although the disease can cause many problems, Wilma's doctors treated her and gave her special medicine that makes the disease less severe. While she is still sick sometimes, Wilma is a strong fighter, just as her name implies. For the most part, she has managed to overcome her health problems.

Wilma did not finish her graduate work, but she continued to work for the Cherokee tribe. She helped the Cherokee people build businesses and find ways of solving community problems. Her most famous achievement is called the Bell Community Project. Wilma helped the town of Bell, Oklahoma, to raise money to bring water pipes into the community. Sixteen miles of water pipes were laid, and for the first time in the town's history, each home had running water. The project also involved restoring several houses to make them livable.

Ross Swimmer, Principal Chief of the Cherokees, was very impressed with Wilma's ability to arrive at solutions to problems and to raise money for projects. In 1983 he had to run for re-election as Chief, and he asked Wilma to run as his Deputy. When they won the election, Wilma became the first woman in the history of the Cherokee tribe to hold the position of Deputy Chief.

Two years later Wilma made history again. Chief Swimmer was selected to join President Ronald Reagan's administration as head of the Bureau of Indian Affairs. When he moved to Washington, D.C., Wilma took over his job. On December 15, 1985, she was sworn in as the first woman Principal Chief of the Cherokees. On the same day, the *New York Times* published an article about her. Wilma was quoted as saying that the Cherokees were concerned "about jobs and education, not whether the tribe is run by a woman or not."

Many Cherokees liked what Wilma did as Chief. In 1987, with her term coming to an end, Wilma decided to see if she could be elected to the position on her own. Although she ran against three opponents—all men—she received an impressive 45 percent of the vote. Under Cherokee law, however, she had to receive 50 percent of the vote in order to win. A runoff election was held between the candidates who'd received the most votes. When all the new votes were counted, Wilma was the winner by more than 1,200 votes. She received 56 percent of the votes cast.

As Chief, Wilma has worked hard to find jobs for unemployed members of the Cherokee Nation, to improve the schools, and to bring better health care to the Cherokee people. She established the Cherokee Nation's Chamber of Commerce to develop businesses in the Cherokee Nation.

Wilma had remarried in 1986. Her second husband is Charlie Soap, a Cherokee who knows the Cherokee language. Because the federal government wanted Indians to adopt the language and culture of the whites, few Indian children now learned to speak their own language. Charlie's knowledge of the language was a great help to Wilma in her election campaign. It probably helped to win over older, more traditional members of the tribe.

Wilma believes strongly that young Cherokees should learn about their tribal culture. An important part of that culture is the Cherokee language. During the summers students attend the Institute for Cherokee Literacy to learn how to read and write Cherokee, using an "alphabet" invented by a man named Sequoyah. After Sequoyah completed the alphabet in 1821, it was adopted for use by the tribe. Within a very short period, thousands of Cherokees could read and write their own language for the first time. Now, after the students learn the language at the Institute, they teach it to other members of the tribe.

Wilma has received many honors and awards. The University of New England gave her an honorary doctoral degree, and she was awarded the Harvard Foundation's Distinguished Service Citation in 1986. A year later in 1987, *Ms.* magazine named her its woman of the year. When she was interviewed for a story in the magazine (January 1988) Wilma said that the Cherokees are treated as though they are "in a museum or a history book." Even people in Tulsa and Oklahoma City, the two largest cities in Oklahoma, Wilma said, did not know that the Cherokees have "a language that is alive, that we have a tribal government that is thriving." Proud of her tribe's accomplishments, Wilma stated, "We have kept the best of our old ways of life and incorporated the sounder elements of today's non-Indian world."

In earlier times, the head of a Native American tribe was responsible for the welfare of the people. The Chief made many decisions that would keep the people from going hungry and safe from danger. In many ways, Wilma's work is the same as the work of past Cherokee Chiefs. She finds ways to bring jobs to her people; she works with the tribal government to keep the community healthy and secure. People in the Cherokee community bring their problems to her, and she helps them to find solutions. Wilma may be the first woman in the history of the Cherokees to serve as Chief, but she is following in a long tradition of leadership provided by the women of the Cherokee tribe.

Although Wilma Mankiller was re-elected Principal Chief in 1991, she does not know if she will continue to be the leader of the Cherokees. She has other goals in her life that she might pursue. She still hopes to finish her graduate-school work. She considers that an important achievement that she would like to carry out. Whatever path she chooses, however, her work will always serve the Cherokee community that she calls home. As she told a reporter for the *Chicago Tribune* (May 14, 1986), "I want to be remembered as the person who helped us [the Cherokees] restore faith in ourselves."

HISTORY OF WILMA MANKILLER

1945	World War II ended. Wilma was born on November 18, 1945, in Tahlequah, Oklahoma.
1957	Wilma's family relocated in San Francisco, California.
1960s	Wilma married and had two daughters.
1969-71	American Indian activists took over and held the abandoned prison on Alcatraz Island. Wilma became active in the American Indian Rights movement.
1976	After her divorce, Wilma returned to Oklahoma with her daughters.
1977	Wilma was employed by the Cherokee tribal government.
1978	Wilma earned a degree in social science from Flaming Rainbow University.
1979	Wilma was seriously injured in an automobile accident.
1983	Wilma was elected Deputy Principal Chief of the Cherokee Nation.
1985	Wilma became Principal Chief of the Cherokee Nation when the Principal Chief resigned. She became the first woman in the tribe's history to hold that position.
1987	Wilma was elected to a full term as Principal Chief of the Cherokee Nation.
1987	Wilma was named *Ms.* magazine's "Woman of the Year."
1991	Wilma was re-elected as Principal Chief.